Hand Over Mouth Music

Hand Over Mouth Music

Janette Ayachi

First published 2019 by
Liverpool University Press
4 Cambridge Street
Liverpool
L69 7ZU

British Library Cataloguing-in-Publication data
A British Library CIP record is available

ISBN 978-1-78694-214-2 softback

Typeset by Carnegie Book Production, Lancaster
Printed and bound in Poland by Booksfactory.co.uk

For my daughters Aria and Lyra: may you each always find your own music

'What are the words you do not yet have?'
Audre Lorde

Contents

I Laughed So Much I Lost My Voice

(i)

Rumour of thunder in my throat, hoarse as a helicopter's
    rusted propellers
still eager for its flight of kamikaze tricks. And I sit in silence
as the owner shouts through to the kitchen from the bar,
makes shadows of chef's repeat orders, her fingers joining the
    dots in the air,
and a constellation of waitresses drop palms full of cutlery,
apologise to each other then everybody else in the room ...
St Andrew Square – buildings inflamed by the stammer of
    their last words.
A fuss of torn cables hammer the air like ruptured arteries,
    then fall limp
under a cargo heap of scrap metal, a landing ceremony of
    mutated stars.
The death rattle dismantling of walls – each brick a sentence
    I lost,
each spinal tap sound of steel plunging at colossal planes of
    glass compensates that loss
as this is the best kind of collision: high-dose, full-throttle,
    alchemical and driven by pulse.
And nothing is left in the rubble except echo, obscenities,
    broken hearts
steeped in the choking smoke of the world's laughter that first
    kidnapped my voice.
I stop to look up, listen to the world and its breaking down
    of things
that were once built to last, as the leaves on the trees suggest
    they, too, have something to say.

(ii)

Married flirtations in public spaces, duets unsteady in liquor
with fate and the endless sky as their audience
ignition of the cardiovascular stirs, as hopeless as I am in
   diamanté
caught in a calibre of denial, a landslide of lovers, these
   moments and no advance
and I have nothing to speak of but love, with no voice to
   unspool its early reaching
a temporary mirage made all the more for its momentary fleet
darkness translates a lesser loneliness, the weight of longing
   left behind
perfume on a pillow, a kite consuming its own shadow
speechless now I let the chorus start marrow beneath
   bone-white
like talking to your unborn child no bigger than peach stone
resilient as botany, or organs pickled in a scientist's bell jar
and the delirious anemone chuckles from its wardrobe of
   stems
makes space in the bed for the muses to raise their voices,
   perform midnight surgeries
women in stitches left with their bodies still strumming their
   string of mistakes
each face on a tripwire journey, spitfire monologues in the
   mirror
slept-on makeup cracking into its own reflection before it's
   wiped clean ....

(iii)

I am more desperate for noise than the dead, a vacant
   drum-kit after a band splits
so I release a soundless scream, bidding my larynx to rise like
   Lazarus

or at least in the same way the rain lifts the streets to silver
just before it snows.
Instead I am gripped, lined up in a dimension of days in the
future
where nothing is mine except my children and my hands
both of which I barely recognise. These sunlit photographs
and discarded dreams, the old woman inside me wrestling to
the surface
as my roots flash a sprouting of railroad grey,
cutting through a scalp of soil like a monocarpic flower in
winter.

(iv)

Was it laughter, an aviary of doubt, that used up all my words
too soon
all this time now to sit hemmed in by silence,
made glamorous behind non-glare museum glass
where the sun remembers nothing of me, nothing even of
itself?
I am muted from the piercing trappings of feeling anything at
all.
I rank my words into order, as numeric as an electricity meter
Frankenstein's first charge – amputated body parts stitched
back to life
centrifugal yet misaligned from the planets,
worryingly insistent on their invisibility.
The unspoken words are saline before morphine,
a cold flush cleansing veins to rid a finesse of sadness
in the sound of a woman crying on the seventh floor of a
tenement,
an ocean set off focus on the screen of an expensive camera,
the toll of church bells on a distant telephone line,
a sunset miming flames, my lover's mouth in every photograph
searched for in every landscape

where songs were played she knew all the words to:

What did you find back there beside the brandishing of
watermarks;

the curlew's first cries, the insomniacs and impresarios of the
heart?

What parts of yourself did you touch, before the chemicals
between us

crystallised to glass and were taken prisoner by the digger's
excitable guillotine?

Aphrodite Hikes Up
Her Skirt in April

The wind lifts my hair like a dreamy lover
drawing coffee steam into her throat

the same way trees and tenements inhale
fog to shift into a brighter afternoon.

I have never been so alone in my life,
running from the bull after teasing it to charge,

my heart defibrillated down a dotted line
of sacred myrtle and diaphanous mirrors.

The only women that matter are the ones
I have to chase like tungsten coil after switch

cooling down to dismantle light in slow motion.
The empty boxes in the calendar remind me

I still have so much space to fill.

On Keeping a Wolf
(for MacGillivray)

Like all the therianthropic women that have tapped
Virgil's sorcerer for his poisonous herbs

I keep the wolf chlorinated with friendship
instead of suffocating her with the trappings of love.

The night we met she appeared straight from the page
of a Gaskell gothic tale with metronome footsteps

fire-proof in lace and velvet
engulfing me like a hurricane on its hind legs.

We leaned into each other over a bar crowd
of people punctuated like rain

our similarities and superstitions centre aligned
we spoke in furious tangential tongues.

Giddy on her smell of clementine peel, argan and tinder
I rested my head back against the chair where I watched

her corset-tight chest rise and fall as she breathed
until brazen-clad in confessional ink we escaped

to smoke cigarettes and kiss.
A feral pawing of retractable flames in doorways.

She invited me to her daylight guise;
an antique bookshop in the Grassmarket,

a fitting cove for a wolf where I clasped her book
like a talisman bulletproof in its hot-print shield

and imagined what the throat of the heart
would sound like after midnight's sober bell.

We played shop, tourists ask for Kipling and whiskey guides.
She tells me where her true love is tied:

to a married man she has known an epoch,
she grinned a charge of stockings and lost boys.

Her pupils Plutonian-dark, as black as my mornings
those last thirty days where grey-haired women walked dogs

picked dandelions and tossed sticks along the river of Lethe.
But here, now, she is the white latex of broken stems;

an old-world language in concertina with the sky,
she is African arrow poison dismantling my pulse

and I am running out of places to hide.

Lawrencium

You were named hastily
barely born from your synthetic subshell
with less than a half-life and so minuscule in volume
but still they pushed you to melting point before your time.
Coming from a long spectral line
of atomic orbitals blocked together as a family
a hot air balloon mirrored in a lake
in the spherical space around the nucleus
you had heritage to spell and highly radioactive secrets to spill
from the accelerated row of beautiful actinides.
What a complex matrix of solvent extraction
all war-torn in dull silver and close-packed hexagons,
oxidised quickly by air, heat and acidic tongues.
You had no chance Sir, though you were more stable
than your siblings who went mad behind other metal doors.
You were made from Russians' bloodied hands
but seized by the proud Americans;
of course you were no cache of gold
yet still they crowned you
in accolade to the inventor of the cyclotron.
Out you spun from high voltage into the royal nuclear arena.
And when they resuscitated you from boron to neon
the lightest and heaviest of your lies
set in alpha decay of your hometown hero Dubnium.
So the spoilt Russians claimed you back as theirs
at the table's head in dark Geneva
where clouds were a slideshow of unhealthy lungs
above a uniform of lab-coats and military gleam:
but by then your tribute title had been too long sealed.
You lost yourself for a while, Lawrencium,
your existence became questionable:

a presumed periodic name remained unsteady.
Then the quick Japanese questioned your position
since you behaved too much like sodium and potassium
this year at the ball of heated tantalums and helium music,
wearing your outer electron, ion suit and the wrong smile.
There is never enough of you to go around all the ladies.
Mostly you are a ghost in the geosphere:
and even science cannot contain you
with all her wealth, prosthetic sunsets, detachable stars.

Falling Asleep On Your Last Memory

But who could blame the birds
when they came, after spent playdates,
popcorn littering the ground like flowering coral
when we sipped prosecco, spun plates
here in the New Town away from the sweat of tenements
and poverty; despite their vandalism and their war cries.

Our children of fables, such ludicrous angels,
each one chooses a weapon and sends a guard to the gates.

Who could blame the birds or embalm their glutton,
those city birds brazen in the capital
like women in floral at the first gape of sun
and how at dawn they flock,
to the over-spilling bins of St John's Cemetery
with a choice of grave worms or fast food.

These birds turn men into stone,
fill Princes Street Gardens with unsuspecting heroes,
put worry dolls in the pockets of prophets,
calm the wretched with their show of kamikaze tricks.

So come birds, see what we have left out for you:
among watermelon pips, ice lolly sticks and tossed up bread;
a banquet of semaphores and secrets, starving hearts and
    dismissed lovers
where windows insist on offering lies, and the sober
    passers-by believe them.

Let your wings graze the cheeks of tourists with an
    undertaker's caress.

Dean Street Gardens

A place where the playpark has a sandpit
and the gates are groomed for secret keys.
Where grandparents walk teenagers in circles,
mothers unhinge over fences
eating air and picking up litter.
Apologies and singing children;
a hairband in absentia on a plateau of grass
and a picnic bench under a liquid canopy of trees.
The clouds hover like gulls over a ghost ship
as if there is always mist to hide in.

Children all crave to be seen.
They destroy sand castles too quickly,
tiny toddlers stamping giant footprints.
'Mum I made a hole, then the hole disappeared'
only the moats remain curving their smiles
through a thicket of Trafalgar-red spades.
Freddie turns a spade into a wand
then turns me into a bear.
Gilbert spills his blueberries, stares at the splatter
as if he were watching them grow.

A man practices chanter-song as he walks his dog
tapping the sheet music with his wedding ring;
and when a playgroup bursts over the horizon
like alien invaders shrouded in neon,
it is only the mothers who think them enemies
as we juggle our snacks and our observations,
look at each other like the sun is always in our eyes.

The kids are mostly happy or unhappy;
forging fond memories as they vanish behind bushes
and sometimes smoke, throw stones at spiders
let ladybirds trapeze-walk across their arms.
And later, when the mothers return home
we watch water boil, feel like magicians ourselves,
clandestine in our midnight veils of moons and stars.

I lock myself in for a while to think;
move the furniture so I can't find the doors or windows,
wear all my keys on chains, all my hearts on mirrors
remembering her stare across the swings
the lust slashed visible through the domestic solidarity
our bond of motherhood, a mound of lionesses.
Her eyes waxy and dark like Whitby jet,
zirconia in the light, more spiced than a shadow
and widening to accept my smile as love arrived in stealth.

Summer of Funerals

During the summer of funerals
I turned myself inwards

tried to understand death
without being vaccinated against it

for the most part I was drowning
in some monumental river

before a stiffened crowd.

Il Piccolo Paradiso

When we walk into her house
        it's as if autumn has swept
                in through the windows
but it is always the heart
        of summer when we visit
                each year for an hour.
Nothing changes over time
        the detritus of plants litter
                dark corners, acorns line
the skirting boards scattered with dust.
Shoebox junk spills over table tops
a Blackadder design replicated
                into gothic, china dolls
seated upright on moth-eaten
        cushions like well mannered
                children facing straw witches
and burlesque puppet clowns.
She sits close to the door
        scratching the table for scum
                in the conversation's silence.
It was the summer of funerals
        after all; when you are old
                death is as familiar as the ache
in your bones. She is deafened
        not by time but by her treasures
                collected from life's cobwebs
the stonewalls plastered
        with fading photographs
                of her only grandson.
Her husband bed-bound for years
        regressing in age, brain-dead
                but body living, kept alive

by her care, monitored by machines.
        We always visit his room.
                Just before we leave,
she lifts his curled hand to salute us.
        The stench is always sour,
                the air unreachable.
His mouth retracts around gums
        the insistence of his jaw juts out
                like a cliff, he is aware
of nothing. His face moon-polished
        like a veteran's medal. We all unfold
                into the garden
landscaping space to live
        alongside the dead,
                filling in our faces with flowers.

Secret Garden in Spring

You take us to your childhood house
its tombstone-marble floors
loose cables knotted in the dark
like pits of rattlesnakes
where upturned cockroaches
collapse under the scent of mould
and stray cats circle the fences
as if they are guarding something valuable.

I take to the garden with our girls
collect five different shades
of rose petals, our hands
cupped with colour, velvet and perfume.
The watery sounds of pigeons distracts us,
a family flock cooing in the gutter,
and Lyra pricks her finger on a thorn.
A perfect speck-circle of blood
swells like an oncoming train from the distance
of an early morning sun.
She squints to magnify the damage,
scope the broken bushes and dead birds
embedded in the margins.

Inside you greet holographs of your parents,
yourself as a young boy
calling out to your friend across a window,
praying at the foot of your bed.
Your fingers twitch for a sign,
or signal, something to show you
what to do after your father's funeral,
some kind of answer for his death.

Spooning Stars

You kept talking about the flame of life
on those visitation days you spent
spooning your father his last meals
of cremated hope and constellations
as his cheeks sunk inwards
and lips curled at the rim
of his teeth where his gums
caught on to the spreading cancer
like catching a secret from an open window.

The crumbs brushed in the silence
when he slept, waking after to ask you
for sangria. You thought he was losing
his mind, his memory, more weight
but he kept a bottle hidden
and you slept beside him
every pitch black night on the ward
where trolley wheels veered under the dead
rubbing your hands for heat
from the last burning embers of his bones
squinting to watch the shiver
                of his dim pulse
as if it pressed upwards against thin skin
like a trapped star searching its exit
                through the needle.

New Mother

One swipe of the sonogram
and the midwife had the sex predicted

she stacked away files like over-sized
tarot cards shuffling through the blood work

slicking the lubricated wand back and forth
like an upturned hourglass to spell out the word

'girl' on the Ouija board of my bulging stomach.
I folded the scan picture like a brewing secret

gave a copy to my mother, the gift of birth passed down
the hands of women, a flat lithograph, grainier

than a memory, a gelatine print,
a boneless x-ray, an alien woodcut.

Not long after that my body shivered
into postpartum, chartreuse light levered

its way through shadows and I became one of the new
mothers wandering the hospital corridors in cotton gowns;

trying on rooms like shoes, barefoot and barren
slotting coins into payphones mechanically calling

future selves to check in, stomachs deflated and slack,
eyes bloodshot like raw steak, darker than forest shadow.

This is the metamorphosis, a new skin shed, the older part
locked in a bathroom somewhere starving and slightly sad

stepping back further into previous chapters
so when the winter strips the trees of their bark

we will stand naked in the mirror
and call out our own names.

Aria

Since my surrender to the cadenza
of the spearminted midwives
you swing inside me like a village hall bell
tugged by the surgeon squire
my legs your tower
the beautiful melody your name.
Aria, your first cry tolls
the opera of the operating theatre halts
a breeze against my mouth.
Clouds crawl in,
your father slightly stooped
like five past six against the face of the sky.

Lyra

The first night you curled in our bed
like a loose semiquaver

I heard aeroplanes descend from the sky;
each crash signalled a siren somewhere

and still you hardly moved, Lyra.
Your feral calm could have muted prophets.

The strings of my heart-shaped harp
ached their first tuneless renderings.

Mummified in the scent of oleander,
my legs knotted in post-birth spasm

like two castle turrets blitzed to rubble.
Your fumble from dark, escape to flashlight

on repeat back to me through the days
that followed where nothing seemed to change

but your increase of hunger
for my free flow of milk.

Survival

In the moon shawl stuttering carriage
with vodka and a gag to mute my curse
my surname was amputated
on the voyage home from surviving war:
so I stitched it back on
and it grew again, stronger muscles flexed.

After your lungs filled their first, Aria,
I hyphenated your father's surname,
a metal plate lodged and locked in place
binding the two sounds, a perfect duet
rooted under sheets of flesh and history
resisting the brittle breakage
of breakup and bone.

Adriatic Sea

Oh Adria, how does it feel to have the Ionian Sea at your heel,
    to hear the lynxes wail at your back from inland Sarajevo,
        or Dubrovnik set spinal tap diagnosing your ailments
and the soft Italian whispers Pescara suckling at your breast?

How does it feel to let Venice reign your cranium
    or to have tidal movements as slight as time?
        The River Po sends over her condolences
in sediment and ceremonial stones
and the Mediterranean thanks you for your freshwater smile.

I know that you spike the marine coast guards to escape at
    night, your waves paralysing as Rohypnol.
        You have lived through the heavy rule of Rome
and owe the Ottoman Empire nothing in its wake.

Costumes hung out as gifts, murder weapons in your girth,
    and Napoleon tasted you sharp in his mouth,
        after securing a shoulder of your shore for Austria.
Those cannon balls and unconscious queens
still wedged in your gut,
fully abundant in flora and fauna
your biodiversity stripped down bare for spitfire.
Nineteen seaports, nineteen peals placed in your garter
all that cargo coming and going, nothing could fracture you.

How many of those leaders did you surprise
    with your thirteen thousand islands rising,
        those sunsets in Croatia, blush in your darkening mirror
waking the Gods with riptide bora gales,
or your premenstrual sirocco storm-related surge
that oscillates your flow with constant tears. Oh sad Adriatic,

how many times have you flooded those myriad conclaves of
    Venice
or collected Saharan sand to cast a spell of rain dust over your
    suitors' eyes?

Clouds from Marseille to Annaba

And in your eyes, father, I see all you try to hide
as you practice your native tongue on the ears of strangers,
that musky smell of hashish familiar on your breath.

You bought me Kafka's *Lettre au Père* to rehearse my French
veiled my face so I would not tempt stray men
and like a widow in mourning I passed through the streets.

I howled in the mirror so the scarf was folded away for after
    my marriage
you flicked through an album of my suitors over coffee and
    croissants.

This is not about revenge, father,
it's about the clouds that carried us back and forth each time

from my head	to your history
my world	to your language
my history	to your world
my language	to your head

and you, not noticing   the distance   in between.

Her Sixties

My mother keeps crossing waters,
I am sure she sails from Scotland to Ireland in her sleep now,
when her eyes seal shut to hollow sockets like loch-washed
    mussels,
eyelashes matted with seaweed, darkened by the rain.
She calls me from friaries, towers, castles, great open plains,
to talk about battles, clearances, the rise and dip of both her
    countries.
Madrigals and ghosts tamper with the line
as she stumbles over the long dead,
a freight-train in the sky quake half-light,
waking ancestors to share their fulcrum of secrets.
Her cloak wavers against some grimoire coastline,
her face bright as a halogen lamp.
When I visit her I see the sea that she crosses
shudder in her eyes, a 'vacancies' sign across her face.
There are rooms now that cannot be filled,
whilst the others clutter dates; history, half-finished canvases,
memories of a miniskirted blue eye-shadowed youth.

So I bring her grandchildren to chase away the archive of
    cobwebs.
She feeds them chocolate and folklore,
starlings dot the spire of her spine
as she wraps herself around their tiny bodies.
I step out of my generation, step back and watch them pull
    closer,
as she unfolds her aloe wings and freckled knuckles over her
    nest.

Graveyard Silence

Waking too early one morning
    the world had stopped moving
        the eternal slide of the clouds
            had arrived at a steadfast halt
                like mother's first paintings
                    the way she dabbled acrylic
on the canvas with a sponge
smothering textures like an unwanted newborn.

Amnesia

The air is heavier   than silver   your eyes
are mentholated blue   flecks   of hawthorn freckle your hair
your fingers are   calloused from the   reins
of time   your thatched wings   let the world
    whistle through   the weight   of you   coming undone
it is a wonder   how you   stand up straight   at all
you look   into the distance   as if you had just
stepped out of someone else's   wardrobe of memories
    scanning the crowds to see   who was   wearing
your own   loss   even the stars   seemed sardonic
    you took steps   with caution   towards
the forever   but you started to feel yourself
come undone   unravelling   like a loose thread
ignored until   half the garment   disappears
      parts of you   lost   in side streets   caught
on doors   or left clinging   to strangers
you attached your emotions   without warning
sometimes   without even noticing   yourself
    you left a   trail   of your   dreams and anxieties
on every corner   fluttering   your weightlessness
into light until   you were almost   invisible
    for so   long   you went unnoticed   avoiding
the scratchy clutches   of the world's wrappings
though in every room you entered   you had
    the saddest eyes   as you started to   feel
yourself   come undone   unfurling   at the edges
like a loose comma   unbinding   even as you   slept
step by   step   you began   to forget   anyone
    you had   ever been   and the stars
have already   started to abbreviate   the word

Valentina Tereshkova

*(A Soviet cosmonaut and the first female
to be flown into space, in 1963)*

My only pet was a canary named after you;
her cage was struck by lightning.
A bird above its wings, as vengeful as a
prisoner parachuting to freedom;
your call-sign code-name was Chaika {Seagull}
embroidered on your space suit,
a lunar crater and a minor planet take your birth title
under their cracked mantles.

A bird inside its wings, as vengeful as a
female pilot parachuting to fame;
after three days in space, weightless and nauseous,
taking photos of the horizon,
a lunar crater and a minor planet take your birth title
into their cracked signature smiles.
From launchpad to unoccupied orbit,
smug in your own utter solitude, empty of song.

Seventy hours in space, weightless and nauseous,
taking photos of the horizon
higher than the entire world,
comets and asteroids spreading a fever of galactic lanterns
that rocketed into orbit smug in their utter solitude,
empty of medals and monuments.
Erected from smooth capsule, bruised, famished
but gifted with a belly of wired butterflies.

Higher than the entire world,
comets and asteroids spread a fever of galactic lanterns.
You toss unable to sleep through the cravings
to speed past those rogue clouds again

counting your ejection from the smooth capsule
on repeat like fence-hopping sheep,
downstairs: a bar full of vodka,
Soviet documents, snaps of a cold wedding in Moscow.

You toss, unable to keep hold of the cravings
to speed past those rogue clouds again
when your double-barrelled daughter dreams
under her cot mobile of the solar system.
Vodka, Soviet documents,
snaps of a cold wedding in Moscow her inheritance,
the roof of the house calmly decorated
with a seagull weathervane keeping watch for storms.

When your double-barrelled daughter dreams
under her cot mobile of the solar system
a lunar crater and a minor planet take her birth title
under their cracked mantles.
In the end you wanted to journey to Mars,
a sacrifice-suicide for one last view of space,
that's why my only pet was a canary named after you
and her cage was struck by lightning.

Father's Biography

Twenty-one years in Algeria rebelling against religion
drinking strong coffee and playing bottle caps
ten years seeking your fortune
three years wearing tight flared trousers
and only dating women with dark eyes
one year in Morocco growing your hair
two years in Italy wielding Fiat cars
and growing your own tomatoes
seventeen years married to my mother
three nights sleeping beside my hospital bed
when I was a sickly child
four years of divorce and threats of burning down the house
while we were sleeping
five years living alone edging insanity and suicide
three years driving back and forth to Scotland
chain-smoking Marlboros
a lifetime in London flicking your cigarette ends
in the same corner
twenty-two years in the same work waiting
tables for celebrities
one year and a half waited on in your arranged marriage
six months content with seeded grapes
and a bride from your birth place
one hour in the car yesterday telling your children
their mother will suffer for taking all your money
twenty-three years smoking hashish in the toilet
twenty-three years watering the same plants
twenty-three years cleaning the same fish tank

many many years never knowing your own grandchildren
and the last years of your life, father, I doubt you will see my
    face.

Ramadan in Annaba

(i)

It is the morning of many sacrifices
      the streets washed with blood
        the sound of sheep stops
           music plays and children cheer
boys carry body parts back to their dens,
smiling hunter-gatherers.

My cousin washes dishes on the concrete
putting cutlery in plastic tubs
like an infant matching up shapes.

(ii)

One boy, just a baby,
carries a head by its horns
the sheep's tongue clamped by its teeth.

Towns become obituaries
      meat on every corner.
        I watch my uncle take a life
           I watch my father, his accomplice
I watch the blood gush from its severed neck.

It watched as I watched
and even in death it watches me.

Flesh under my father's fingernails
on my way home in the car to the airport.

Shame in the Family

After a while, like the sky to the moon, she became oblivious
until the sea offered reflection. Her umbilical cord a stubborn
    shooting star.
She housed her, her weight and routine metamorphosis
immune to her presence, though almost full she hung in her
    uterus
speaking in tongues when her nights were thick like tar.

After a while, like a weasel to its scrap yard home, she became
    oblivious
to the smell of gasoline or the surrounding trees of eucalyptus
when she killed more than she could eat, death dancing in circles
    at the altar.
Speaking in tongues when her nights were thick like tar.
The child grew accustomed to her and her mind grew more
    vacuous,
she fed on her residue and one day she strayed out too far.

After a while, like breath to the ear, she became oblivious
to the echo of her escape-cry tossing in and out of nebulous.
A labouring language to fathom, though she translated the word
    daughter.
She fed on her residue and one day she strayed out too far.

Her body yawned from the middle a viscous plant carnivorous
crying out from honey gland placenta for its own feed of flies and
    rain water.
After a while ebbing the slow shutdown of life she became
    oblivious.
A labouring language to fathom, though she translated the word
    daughter.

Youma and the Three Kings

The imam, a witch doctor and the local visionary
arrive like three kings hovering with offerings,
they fold and stretch in silhouette, light incense
shrouded in spells and prayers, swinging amulets,
clinking sacks of ruin stones, spitting into potions.
Their healing hands cupping mist and the half-dark.

They all knew each other like a secret
bowing into houses with their curious whispers
to save the living or wave away the dead
with royal blood, holy water, dirges and second sights.

Youma surrendered her weight to their presence
she watched the beaded curtain dance in the doorway
where a weave of light eclipsed the cement floor
to settle like a gauze draped over her skin.

I was bound to the vortices of voodoo, kismet, curse,
this premonition of how she would look two days later
after my flight back home, when the undertaker would offer
her last gift wrapping her in a silk-thread muslin before
burial.
The three kings hovering in the background
absolutely still in silhouette.

Youma and the Moon

The medallion moon looped itself
through a threadbare ribbon of cloud
fixed in place by the fingerprints of night
and snapped shut in the velvet box of the sky.

Inside I watched her unravel her headscarf
fingering, fumbling, slow, meticulous
like uncovering an ancient tomb.
She pressed the perspiration
away from her temples
her hair once henna-gold now a dull coin
lifted from its burial purse of sand and dust.

A black pebble was placed beside her bed
when she was no longer able to wash
its oily sheen like an Oban seal
reflecting the moon's glare.
It stole solar light
to comfort her as she tossed in fever
as alley-cats scratched the corrugated roof.

She stroked its greasy head as if water sluiced
from the stone and carried imaginary drops
to her parched body, then withered back
under sheets like a sun-sapped weed   /
or salted snail repellent to its shell.
The light no longer reached her corner.
Family came to hold her curled hand in the dark.

Outside the sea gloriously
chanted the names of all it drowned.
It was then for the first time 'youma' sounded
only like a murmur and the moon was handed out
in   pieces   like   all   of   her   gold.

What She Saw

You never wore a patch in your last years, Youma,
the absent eye always exposed
as age unravelled the body's secrets.
There was nothing left to hide,
the skin sunk in the centre
a stubborn soufflé resisting to rise,
the muscle of your mouth flexed into a frown.

Always bent in corners peeling vegetables,
separating pulses or kneading *kissera*,
the floor stove between your legs,
the gas flex curled up your skirt like a catheter.
Many years of draining your heart into your food
had left you hollow.

You were never warm and loving,
never cuddled, never sang, never cried,
still we all tenderly called you 'Youma'.
You were 'mother' to all, an immortal matriarch
in the background of every family photograph,
plaits gilded to your head like armour
a statue, a shadow, the centre of our tribe.

I know now that without turning your head
the other side of the world
just never existed.
In the end stepping away from your life
was like stepping back from a painting
to gain the only perspective
your sights had ever known.

Everything Is Diminished
Without You In It

I lived in a dream where faith had been disconnected;
a burning Arab woman with a face full of painted eyes
'cover your ankles', said my father, *'have you no shame?'*
as I reached the pirate smile of the man I was to marry,
'you finish your studies then you will live here'.
I imagined what I would carry across the underworld.
I found solace on those igneous nights
when the wind crept up from the sea
and the women crept away from their beds
to congregate in the hammam after midnight;
nakedness now, hair unveiled as seamless as the Sahara
and slowly released like steady gunfire.
Hammam or haram, I pondered, as the steam depleted all
    disguises
blood ran freely and flesh announced its electricity.

I tipped against the voluptuous swarm
of sunbombed women who would later all rise,
all rise, all rise, then kneel for morning prayer,
this curse of what one inherits and how through life it scowls.
Love is like this; a rain cloud that dances with her own shadow,
kicks the covers off at night to sleep, as rife as potassium.
From downpour to spittle, great floods to bleaching drought,
what do we really take from those moments of closeness;
the length of her fingers across my ribs
at a time, we know no more than this, the healing properties
    of breath
and her paradisiacal mouth against my lips.
Mouths press together, this is how it happens, you are already
    leaving.

Walking After Midnight

What is this country
        that I return to
                for answers

native to me
        only in snippets
                but most familiar

when night shakes
        its black cape
                and the decade's dust
disseminates into stars.

The stars show me
        wounds of love tonight;
                silver bullet holes
piercing the surface,
        clogged arteries
                in constellations,
gluttonous desire
        in streaming blood.
                The jagged red
        cusp of my heart
                wants you near.

Hand Over Mouth Music

It is the ceremony of my father's second wedding.
    The entire brooding family gather
        to clean, cook, arrange the celebration.

Women huddle in corners
    bending and twisting under long robes.
        Some sway like the tide as they wash
        the floor with rags.

The lonely satellites of their eyes repeat
    a gaze passed down through generations,
        a way of looking at the world.

The women stay close together
    exhausted, pregnant,
        bleeding in each other's arms.

They have their music, hand over mouth
    tongue under teeth, a sound they put to songs,
        a siren sound they wrap themselves
        around.

This is their blues, a work song without words, one call and
    they all chorus.

The men smoke and shout and smack their children,
    are waited on like kings; feasts of fruit prepared.
        I watch my father's new bride

preparing the night in the dark alcove of her bedroom,
    removing her bodily hair. Nobody minds my
        presence, they want me to learn.

She swabs herself in rubies, paints her face, nakedness,
        lotions, perfume mixes with the smell of onions,
                olive oil and I step outside for fresh air.

Father follows to tell me that our next visit will be my
        wedding then kisses the top of my head
                before going back inside to shadow.

Hand over mouth I stand with salt on my lips
        staring at the blurring hands of old men
                who play cards in dust under the stars.

Sauchiehall Street

Sauchiehall Street is space-blue and silver in winter
her alien-hex skin pressed with diamonds and dust,

her slick vertebrae makes way for the applause of cars
where a therapy of ignition tracks her spine

to spill champagne and socialists,
tranquillise pedestrians, run ladders in pre-war stockings.

In summer she gives you that look, someone horn-struck
and about to undress in front of you, so you blank out

all the side streets, concentrate on her striptease.
On those nights she reaches for lovers

seduces them under her skirt of shuttered shops;
velvet saunas, skyscraper hotels, cocktail hours.

This street is more hysterical than historical,
as most women tend to be marked,

her lips too numb for kisses so she spits
into the mouth of pollution, swallows traffic cones.

When bleached by the gulf of self-loathing
she lets knives flash under her streetlamps,

bends to gear violence into her palm
like loosened fruit still sore from its secular branch-snap

prone to flex post-mortem.

She hordes the hooligans in their hoods,
samples a taste of their furious hunger,

holds them the same way stags grip
those wretched birds of paradise in their midnight antlers.

Oh Sauchiehall Street you are a hall of mirrors
with your music-hall name delivering illusion!

Glasgow's graceless steps palpitate towards
stampede to unhinge your promised land,

shadows display a promenade of romances
on *The Locarno Ballroom* dance floor.

The sad bottled eyes of French girls
in polyester on their way to Kelvingrove

awake in clusters with their faces
creased like abandoned linen

dizzy from the smell of cordite in their dreams.

This street is not a language
or a place to salvage euphoria,

oh no, there is a helpful smile in every aisle
if you trust the magician's saw

and newsreaders on every corner
to renegade tomorrow's cry of surrogate heroes.

Her signposts promote neutrality to scaffold the future,
because despite bomb blasts

Mackintosh still coloured tearooms with stained glass
and Art Deco reigned-over posh shops,

luncheon frills, high-end theatres where Sinatra sang
those years after open-air suffragettes

paraded taffeta and no surrender
or cadmium orange tramcars ivory trim

plum dashes that pulsed over cobbles –
the internal grits and gifts of life.

A gold-gilded cinema-mad city, smokeless, slow, burning.

Princes Street Gardens

Suitcases and empty shoes
on the grass in Princes Street Gardens;

a boy takes pictures of himself
in the shade under an oak tree

lovers massage each other, fiddle with hair,
talking and kissing too much.

Two hours split from work
and I place myself in a photograph;

the city behind us, summer smoothes the creases
as we roll up our trousers

stretching ourselves out like starfish
floating on a sea of grass blades and dead blossom.

But suddenly there was stillness.
The sun snuck behind a sulking cloud,

a football missiled so high it seemed to stop mid-air,
nothing moved except the leaves on the trees

until two children flung themselves down slopes
like acrobats dismantling the pyramid

and everything started rolling again
shapes reformed shadows pulsed, people cheered,

and at that moment you did not colonize my thoughts,
I was rid of your last smile, quivering, lipstick smeared.

Closed Doors

My crush on you has taken us here
to the mechanical failure of lifts
in Edinburgh's National Gallery.

We kiss all tongues in our borrowed time
where only the mirror tells the truth
and our weight shifts.

The pulley instigates flight until
doors open like a dropped book
spilling its forbidden pages.

Birds of Passage

Each day is a bird
every tomorrow is still caged
yesterday never returns
to tell us there is land beyond the flood.

Most days have broken wings
and do not take flight at all
instead they march mindlessly
in circles around the cage.

Sometimes days fall mid-flight
flapping and convulsing
as they find the ground
and lose their nest.

Today plunged into the world
sucking air into its tiny lungs
screeching as it smashed the skyline
with its flustered wings.

Monday was a canary with its bright beginning
Tuesday was a parrot that never stopped talking
Wednesday was a nightingale that stunned me with its lullaby
Thursday had not hatched so I stayed in bed
Friday was an owl howling its stentorian toot for the weekend
Saturday is an eagle swooping down to hunt with its keen vision
Sunday is still asleep.

God the bird watcher with his binoculars
Creating seven days and counting feathers.

Djinn

Sahara tribes in paradise
in a town I was named after,

burying bread to bake
in the hot sand.

Camp fires boil their sweet tea
and everyone stays up late singing.

Women in tents
suckling, making clothes;

a French reporter
smiling in her strange headdress

foreign to her face,
crossing the divide.

Delta of Italy

Two rainbow arcs
      Format a circle
           Around the sun
Its corona bond
      Stimulates a life
           Seeking a strata
In the climate's pause.

The seething sun
      Will always transfer
           Its slow novocaine
To the restless souls.
      Who can resist
           Such a stasis
Of healing chrysalis.

Merchant City

I like it here – the radiator and music booms, the waitress wears trouser-braces, her mouth the most alluring pout as she shakes a margarita. Two girls on a nearby sofa hold hands and talk about the song. I watch their fingers closely.

Already I know who is the loved and who the lover. One dances at the bar with a bottle of beer trying to impress, acting like she knows she is being watched. The other locks into her phone. Red strobe-glow spills from each table's candle, the bar on fire with plastic stars, and everywhere else is shadow.

A few men dressed in heels and long-sleeved gloves sling shots in profile into false eyelashes, speech bubbles and glitter. Blue lights seep in from the outside – the stars now clotted in puddles. Two hours go by and mirrors have appeared, have appearances, and then disappear. I lose myself in the flood of fairy-lights and couples. I wait for you even when I discover you won't be coming.

Siphon
(For PC)

Snare on the fourth pulse
    you take me underwater

        where the shadows of sharks
            graze forgotten shipwrecks

the heart all petrol spill, androgen and tempo
    synthesized, diaphanous lungs

        and we are in that bar again
        all tongue-tied then tipsy

in the Neptunian-dark of the date's end.

    My fingers press into your body
half-expecting to surface on the other side

    thread-through like a nail-slit daisy chain
palm-temperature, fit for ceremony.

    A scriptorium of futuristic mannequins
line the main street windows facing home:

    a faint nimbus of sub-serrated rainstorm
illuminates a planetarium of medusae,

    your scent over my clothes
siphons to meet my pillow's last lullaby

    and my mouth keeps me awake
with the prophecies scored in braille by our kiss.

St Kilda
(For DM)

One o'clock gun adrenaline shoots the virtual worlds' Technicolor
   vulgarities –
but it's all her   the passionate kisses in bars by rivers in the rain
   the blur of the world
where transportation shape-shifting and possession are all
   triggered
when I am high she is passively affected   when she panics I calm
   her down
when I am vulnerable she flatters me   so I dive in heart first at
   the deep end
feel the rush when the destination is bottomless
the point of reach carries a double cello echo and I tense up over
   my panic for oxygen
did my chest borrow enough weight for the voyage
I trust it to fall fathoms like the gold-plated siren on the face of a
   ship
drowning in emotional wreckage   we will just keep falling
facing each other   yin and yang   twins in embryo
would one of us survive if the anchored umbilical is unchained
   from ankles
soon this place will be too small   my many lives topple
suggestive in the wind   maddening in the quiet   then
   monochrome in memory.
My mouth between her legs and when she tightens   flexed with
   pleasure
a snake preparing to swallow its prey
and I am that siren again drowning off the coast of St Kilda
she is taking pictures in Kelvingrove Gallery for her class
   shadows are furious on film
the old chests of the last inhabitants as they smuggled their lives
   off the island

stuffed gannets and puffins stiff forlorn and less real   than their
    ghosts
of bullet-wounded archipelago cats   a lonely life
but she never once thought that for a minute   its emptiness
    thrilled her
like stepping onto another planet she craved a visit   to cross the
    treacherous waters
not knowing if she would make it back   or remain stranded in
    that solar stillness
                                left talking in tongues to the city
    lights in her sleep.

Whale-Bone and Blood-Letting

'In the midst of winter, I found there was,
within me, an invincible summer'

Albert Camus

I have spent the short summer days
    scanning the treasure in the tan skin

that finds its first wrinkles, searching all
    all of the sea's calm and calamities

that negotiate behind the eyes' thin cellophane.
    In the background there are wars

a thousand screens of the universe, manipulated images
    set to self-destruct in mentally fumed living rooms.

I switched off the world; its synopsis, headlines,
    heavy lies, false maps. Oceans were toxic;

parents turned on their children, riots ruled over capitals,
    waves wiped out consensus, strangers united in rubble

pulling up what was left of their lives
    from the residual lives of other people.

Medals, shoes, water-damaged photographs,
    a brocade of material existences

the vaulted throat of the afterlife
    coughed out an emission of our spent jewels.

At times like this madness could have crept in so easily,
    a depression as deciduous as plants.

The mackerel sheen of night coats the sky,
    recurring dreams of whale-bone and blood-letting,

the mind offers the body a sword, a shield of wire-netting.
    I wait for the sharp claws of winter –

holding the appetite of the sun still panting within me
    the dry roots of the evergreen confirm nothing but thirst.

Sea-Rattle

The sound of the sea reaches our tenement tonight
tides curve their tails around towering brickwork
chasing pipework in circles, staining windows
with rims of salt, seeping in to rot the floorboards.
The mice make boats out of bone-china teacups,
stream towards sewers licking their whiskers.
The light in our room radiates; challenges moonshine,
signals ghost ships, throbs like an endomorphic heartbeat.
I hear the hammering of planks in the stairwell
the guttural pull of the sea's sweeping swell,
two-by-two in miniature diptychs the neighbours escape
abandoning hope and their biodegradable materials
for the bounty of blue, starlight and the promised land.
I bolt my doors as the paint starts to peel;
a flock of gulls crash their beaks against glass,
the sea rattles then roars, furniture soon floats
to the ceiling. Like a spell water funnels up the chimney,
light sizzles then burns out, moons flag on the horizon.
I start to wonder how long before everything is engulfed.
The fumes are quick, eyes adjust to the sting,
lungs inflate and learn to speak. I hold my breath,
listen to their oscillations and swim towards the sky.

Acknowledgments

Thanks to the editors of the following publications where some of these poems first appeared:

A Choir of Ghosts (Calderwood); *Best British Poetry 2015* (Salt); *Dear Watson: The Very Elements of Poetry* (Beautiful Dragons Press, Berlin); *Gutter*; *Literary Mama California*; *Mslexia magazine*; *New Writing Scotland* (Glasgow University); *Not Just A Drop: Just Oceans of Poetry* (Beautiful Dragons Press, Berlin); *Oxford Poetry* (Oxford University); *Poetry Scotland*; *Scotia Extremis*; *Spoke: New Queer Voices*; *Sweat and Tears*; *Umbrellas of Edinburgh: Poetry and Prose from Scotland's Capital City* (Freight); *Writing Motherhood* (Seren).

Gratitude in abundance to Deryn Rees-Jones, Rob A. Mackenzie and JL Williams for their surgeon-precision cuts stitches and edits to this book. And I would also like to thank my tribe of artists; my fellow poets, my mother, my bloodsisters, my soulsisters, and Caroline Fulton for our letters and glorious soundboard for language. Each of whom have supported, infuriated and inspired me in some way. I love you all as much as I love immensely hot sunsets when even under dark skies the earth keeps radiating heat. I am compassed by a circle of strong creative women, which has always helped gear my flight.